The White Moose

By Betty Waterton

Illustrated by David Craig

Jaap Tuinman

CONSULTANTS
Anna Cresswell
Gail Heald-Taylor
Lynda Hodson
Glen Huser

ADVISER
Moira McKenzie

PROGRAMME EDITOR
Kathleen Doyle

Schofield & Sims Ltd
Educational Publishers

Journeys
Level Five
The White Moose

TEACHER CONTRIBUTORS
Barbara Currie
Jay Milne

ISBN 0-7217-0563-4

Printed and bound in England
ABCDEFGHI 9876543210
First printed 1985

ART/DESIGN CONSULTANT
Hugh Michaelson

TYPESETTING
PFB Art & Type Ltd.
FILM
Colourgraph Reproduction Systems Inc.
PRINTING
Chorley & Pickersgill Ltd.

The White Moose

This story is about an animal called a moose which lives in North America. The same animal is called an elk in Northern Europe.

The sun shone warm and golden through Billy's bedroom window. He lay still for a minute, listening to the morning sounds of the farm. Then he quickly pulled on his clothes and ran down to breakfast.

"I'm going to the marsh today," he told his mother. "I want to catch some tadpoles."

"Sounds fine to me," Mrs. Larson said. "Just don't forget about your chores."

Billy nodded, his mouth full of food.

After breakfast, Billy went out to the chicken-house. There were seven eggs, the most he'd found all week. Then he filled his arms with firewood and carried it into the house. It was Billy's job to fill up the wood-box beside the big kitchen stove every morning.

He made himself a sandwich and put it into one of his overall pockets. He stuffed an apple into the other. Then, grabbing an empty honey jar to put the tadpoles in, he ran off across the hayfields.

Tall bulrushes grew around the edge of the marsh, and there were yellow water lilies in the middle. On the far side were willow trees and beyond those, the forest.

Billy stood watching at the edge of the marsh. A blue kingfisher dived into the water and swooped out again with a fish in its bill. Bright dragonflies darted back and forth across the water, their wings humming softly. A family of black and white ducks paddled by. They had been there for some time, and now the ducklings were almost as big as their mother. There were lots of tadpoles, too.

Suddenly, Billy got a funny feeling—as if something were watching him. "A bear!" he thought. As slowly as he could, Billy turned his head. "Wow!" he said softly to himself.

There, white and huge against the dark trees of the forest, was a moose. A *white* moose!

Billy couldn't believe his eyes. He had never seen or even heard of a white moose before.

The white moose stood watching Billy, his eyes bright and curious. He was so close that Billy could see the velvety fuzz on his wide antlers.

Billy wondered why the moose didn't run away. They stood staring at each other for a long time.

Billy remembered the apple in his pocket. Very slowly, he took it out and put it on the ground. Then he slowly backed away.

The moose stepped forward. He lowered his great heavy head to sniff the apple, then he bumped it with his humpy nose. Finally, the moose picked the apple up in his mouth and began crunching it.

"Wow!" said Billy again.

The moose walked into the water and began to pull up big clumps of lily roots. He stood feeding for a long time.

Billy sat on the bank, watching. The moose's white coat gleamed in the sun. When the moose lifted his great head to look at him, Billy thought, "You know I'm your friend, don't you?" Billy felt very happy.

At last the moose turned and waded out of the marsh toward the willow trees. Soon he disappeared back into the forest.

Billy forgot all about catching tadpoles. He ran across the fields, whistling and singing all the way home.

That week he went every morning to the marsh and waited for the white moose . . . and every morning the white moose came.

At last Billy could keep his secret no longer. He told his mother and father about the moose. "And I'm his friend!" he said proudly.

"A white moose! Impossible!" said his father. "You've seen moose before, Billy—they're brown."

"But this one's white!" cried Billy.

"Maybe it's a magical moose," his mother said softly. "I read once that in India, when a white elephant is born, people say it's magic!"

Billy wasn't sure that his mother and father really believed there was a white moose, so the next morning he took them to the marsh.

"Be very quiet," he said, "or you'll frighten him away!"

They waited and waited. The sun climbed higher and higher, until it was right overhead. It was noon and still the white moose hadn't come.

"I'm sorry, Billy," said Mr. Larson, "but we can't wait any longer."

Billy's mother and father went back to the farm, but he stayed on, watching the forest and waiting.

"I guess it's only me he comes to see," said Billy.

But still the white moose didn't come. "Maybe he's never coming back," he thought sadly.

Then, just when he was giving up hope, the white moose appeared! He glided silently out of the forest, his ears wig-wagging as he looked at Billy.

Billy was so excited that he walked right up to the moose, holding out the apple he'd brought. The white moose took it! His mouth felt soft and whiskery on Billy's hand.

"Mum was right!" whispered Billy. "You are magical!"

He ran all the way home, leaping and bounding across the fields, not stopping until he reached the farmhouse. "He came!" shouted Billy. "He came!"

That night Mrs. Larson said, “There’s a medicine show in town tonight. Shall we go and see it?”

Billy had never been to a medicine show.

“It’s like a travelling carnival,” explained his mother. “They have music and there are magic acts. Sometimes there are even wild animals.”

Billy’s eyes were round and shining. Magic! Wild animals!

He rode into town in the back of the little pick-up truck. Bumpety-bump they went over the dusty roads. Billy leaned against some bags of feed and looked up at the sky. It was slowly getting dark and the stars were coming out. One by one, their twinkling lights began to shine through the deep blue summer sky.

The medicine show was set up in a field near town. There was a big red wagon with the words *Captain Smiley's Medicine Show* painted on it in fancy gold letters. There were rows of benches filled with people and a stage lit with bright lanterns.

On the stage stood a tall man with big black whiskers. He wore a red coat with gold braid. He was talking in a loud voice.

"Step right up, ladies and gentlemen! Don't be shy! Find a seat and watch the show! There's lots of room up here in front!"

He smiled right at Billy and winked. Billy smiled back.

"That must be Captain Smiley," whispered Billy. "Can we sit in the front row?"

"Certainly!" laughed his father. "Why not!"

Soon the show began. First, there was a man who played the fiddle while another man sang. The songs were funny and Billy liked them.

Then Captain Smiley did some magic tricks. He pulled dozens of silk scarves, all knotted together, out of his coat sleeve. He whisked them over his head and —POOF!—they all came undone!

"Did you see that?" cried Billy as the scarves floated down all over the stage.

"I'll need a helper for my next trick," said Captain Smiley. He looked down at Billy. "How about you, young man?"

His face all pink, Billy stood up on the stage in front of everyone while Captain Smiley took a silver dollar out of his ear. Then he gave the dollar to Billy.

When Billy sat down again, he opened his hand to look at the dollar. It had turned into a nickel! How had Captain Smiley done that?

After that, Captain Smiley began to sell his bottles of medicine. *Smiley's Magic Elixir*, he called it. Only a few people bought the bottles, but everybody stayed in their seats. They were waiting to see the wild animals.

At last it was time. There turned out to be only one wild animal—a dancing bear. Captain Smiley led it around the stage a few times, but the bear didn't seem to want to dance.

When the medicine show was over, Captain Smiley jumped down from the stage. "Well, young man," he said to Billy, "how did you like the show?"

"It was great!" exclaimed Billy. "But where did my silver dollar go?"

"Ha!" said the Captain. "That's a secret! I know lots of tricks—why, if I touched your nose right now, I could turn it into a carrot!"

Billy put his hand on his nose.

"Don't worry," laughed Captain Smiley, "your nose is safe!"

"I liked the bear the best," said Billy. "You know, I've got a moose at home—a white moose!" Billy found himself telling all about the moose.

Captain Smiley listened carefully. "Where did you see it?" he asked. "Does it come every day?"

He looked over at Billy's mother and father. "Have you folks seen this white moose too?"

Billy's father shook his head. "Well, no . . . we haven't."

"But you have, haven't you?" said the Captain, patting Billy on the head. "Do you think I could come out to see it?"

"Sure," said Billy, "come tomorrow. In the morning."

Then Captain Smiley took Billy behind the red wagon to see the bear. Billy wanted to know all about him. "How old is he?" he asked. "What does he eat?"

The Captain gave a short laugh and said, "Too old and too much."

Billy watched the bear. He was in a cage now, pacing back and forth. He looked so much smaller than when he was up on the stage. His eyes were sad—not bright and curious like those of the moose. Billy wondered if the bear ever dreamed at night about being back in a dark green forest. "Poor bear," thought Billy.

Then Captain Smiley said, "I'd really like an animal like that white moose of yours for my show."

All at once, Billy was sorry that he'd told Captain Smiley about the moose.

That night he couldn't get to sleep for a long time. He kept thinking about the sad eyes of the bear. He couldn't let Captain Smiley take the white moose!

The next morning Billy got up very early. He put on his coat and slipped quietly out of the back door. The sun was just coming up pink and red in the east. The air was cool and there was a white mist hanging over the land as Billy headed across the fields.

The blackbirds were already singing their morning songs when he got to the marsh. Swallows were swooping overhead catching insects.

But the white moose was not there.

Billy sat down and waited. After a while, he heard the snap of a twig being broken. He turned around, and there at the edge of the forest, was the white moose.

Billy jumped up. "No!" he shouted. "Go away! Go away!" He ran at the white moose, waving his arms and shouting. "Go back into the forest! It's not safe for you here! Go!"

The moose looked puzzled. His head was high, his ears were forward, and his nostrils quivered. Billy saw a strange glow in his eyes.

For one awful minute, Billy thought that the moose might charge at him, and he was afraid.

Then suddenly, the moose turned and trotted away, back into the shadowy forest.

Billy watched him go. “And don’t come back!” he yelled. Then he picked up a stone and threw it into the forest. All at once, everything was quiet—not even the blackbirds sang.

Billy sat down on the ground and cried.

"Billy, I saw your white moose. He was beautiful!" Billy turned around to see his father standing behind him.

"That was a very brave thing you did. I'm proud of you!" Mr. Larson hugged Billy. At last Billy stopped crying. Then he took his father's hand, and together they began to walk back across the fields towards the farmhouse.

"Captain Smiley won't get him now, will he, Dad?" Billy asked.

"No," said Mr. Larson. "The white moose is safe now."

Billy nodded. "Do you think he might come back to the marsh some day?"

"Well, you never can tell about a moose."

Billy smiled up at his father. "Especially a *white* moose!" he said.